W9-CTL-582

100 WAYS
TO SAVE
THE PLANET

WITHOUT
LEAVING THE
NEIGHBORHOOD

Managing Editor: Simon Melhuish
Series Editor: Nikole G Bamford
Designer: Stephen Godson

Published by The Lagoon Group
PO Box 311, KT2 5QW, UK
PO Box 990676, Boston, MA 02199, USA

ISBN: 978-1-906170-36-3
© LAGOON BOOKS 2007

All rights reserved. No part of this publication
may be reproduced, stored in a retrieval
system, or transmitted in any form or by any
other means electronic, mechanical,
photocopying or otherwise, without prior
permission in writing from the publisher.

www.thelagoongroup.com
Printed in China

100 WAYS

TO SAVE THE PLANET

WITHOUT

LEAVING THE

NEIGHBORHOOD

Other titles in this series

100 Ways to Save the Planet
without Leaving the House

100 Ways to Save the Planet
without Leaving the Office

100 Ways to Save the Planet
without Breaking a Sweat

1. Join your local library.
Don't buy books if you don't need to — you can order most titles from your local library.

2. Stop buying newspapers.

You can read them in your local library or online.

3. Buy organic cotton clothes.

They use far less resources than standard cotton, so you can truly bless your cotton socks.

4. Research electrical products before buying them. Efficient appliances are labeled with energy ratings and will save money as well as electricity over the course of their life.

5. Service your car regularly.

An efficient engine uses less fuel and if you remember to ensure your tires are inflated to the correct pressure, the engine will not have to work so hard.

6. Shop locally.

Reduce pollution and congestion by walking or cycling to your local shop rather than driving to supermarkets.

7. Make your own beer or wine.

Kits are getting cheaper all the time, and you'll be doing your bit by avoiding all the cost of brewing and transportation — not to mention the cans and bottles.

8. Bank ethically.

Switching your bank account has never been easier, so do a bit of research and move your money to a bank that has a sound ethical policy. Make sure you inform your old bank why you are switching.

9. Walk.

Most car journeys are for distances of under two miles — get fit and help save the planet at the same time.

10. Buy a bike.
For slightly longer journeys, a bike is a much quicker alternative than walking, and will still help you get fit.

11. Don't go automatic.
A car with a manual gearbox is generally more fuel-efficient than an automatic. If you don't know how to drive a manual, or your skills are rusty, then take a few lessons — it's easier than you think.

12. Switch to a hybrid car.

These are now widely available and use an electric battery when you are nipping around town. If you must use a petrol car then see Tip 13.

13. Switch to a smaller car.

Most people don't need a big
gas-guzzler to get about
and smaller cars are much more
comfortable than in days
gone by.

14. Make a shopping list.

If you make a list of what you need, you'll be less likely to buy too much or to buy things that later go to waste.

15. See the light.
A wind-up torch is perfect for power cuts or just finding your way down to the basement.

16. Separate your recycling.

If you're using a bottle bank, for example, don't just lump the different colored bottles into the same bank. Mixed colored glass is less valuable than glass that has been separated into different colors.

17. Don't throw it out.
If you have old clothes or books
that you no longer require then
donate them to a charity shop.

18. Take a bag with you when you go shopping.
Plastic bags just end up in landfill and can take many years to degrade — take your own bag with you and reuse any bags you already have.

19. Buy fruit and vegetables loose.

You don't need to put fruit and vegetables into separate plastic bags — buy them loose and wash them before use.

20. Don't hose your drive.

Use a broom to sweep your drive and paths instead.

21. Seek out your local police auctions.

The police often sell off unclaimed property — bicycles are very common — so find out when the next auction is in your area and see what you can pick up second-hand before you rush out to buy anything new.

22. Don't drive your children to school.

If at all possible, walk your children to school or get them a bike if they are old enough. If it is completely impractical not to drive, then perhaps share the school run with another parent.

23. Swap magazines.

Rather than buying a whole raft of magazines every week, team up with a friend or colleague and agree to swap any titles you both enjoy.

24. Buy quality clothes.

It may cost a little more to invest in good quality clothes, but you will recoup the money if the garment lasts years rather than months — and you'll be helping the planet by using less resources.

25. Get a good butt.

Use a rain butt to collect rainwater for tasks such as watering the garden. It saves water, and the rainwater is generally better for your plants.

26. Take a cutting.
If you admire a neighbor's
plants, ask them if you can
take a cutting, and grow a new
plant from this. Many plants
sold in shops have traveled
vast distances and so used
precious resources en route.

27. Buy organic food.
Whenever you can afford to,
choose the organic option —
pesticides can be harmful to
both the planet and yourself.

28. Let a section of your garden grow wild.

Weeds, wild flowers and nettles will attract all manner of beneficial insects into your garden — and they'll take care of many common garden pests for you.

29. Join a toy library.

Children quickly get bored with toys, so borrow them from your local toy library and then hand them back when little Johnny moves on to the next 'must-have' toy.

30. Go for glass.

Whenever possible, choose products that come in glass containers rather than plastic ones. And, of course, recycle your glass!

31. Use nature's larder.

If you are lucky enough to live close to where wild berries grow, then pick as many as you can while they are in season. They'll taste far better than the ones in the shops, and the only transport cost will be your own shoe leather.

32. Get on to someone.

If you see a streetlight left on during the day, or a pipe that is leaking water, contact your local authority and let them know. The situation will never improve if no-one knows about it.

33. Use a trigger nozzle on your garden hose.

Ideally use rainwater rather than water from the mains supply, and fit a trigger nozzle onto your hose so that you don't waste water as you move around the garden.

34. Get an allotment.
It costs buttons to get your own allotment, and once you have one you can grow your own vegetables rather than buying them from the shop. They'll taste better, cost nothing — and you'll get fit in the process of growing them.

35. Burn a citronella candle.

Don't use electric mosquito repellents or coat yourself in chemicals — wear a long-sleeved top and burn a more environmentally-friendly citronella candle to keep mosquitoes and other buzzing nasties away.

36. Move a mole.
If you have a problem
with moles, you can get rid
of them the green way by
putting a few cloves of garlic
in the molehills.

37. Quit the gym.
You can easily keep fit
without visiting buildings
that require heating,
air conditioning and cleaning.

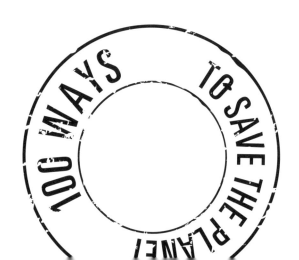

38. Turn the key and go.

Don't start the car's engine and then rummage around for CDs, sunglasses or whatever. Only start the engine when you are really ready to set off.

39. Heal your old shoes.
There's no need to throw out
shoes just because the soles
are wearing thin — in most
cases you can easily have the
shoes re-soled.

40. Hunt down arrowroot wallpaper.
Arrowroot plant is fast-growing and renewable, so it is much more environmentally-friendly than traditional wallpaper.

41. Install double glazing.
Or, better still, triple glazing.
This will lower your
energy consumption, and make
the world seem a little
quieter too.

42. Reheat with a microwave.
If you need to reheat leftovers, use a microwave rather than a conventional oven. Microwaves use far less energy, so use them when you can.

43. Empty your car.

Don't drive around with half your possessions in the back of your car — you'll improve fuel economy if the car is lighter.

44. Visit a friend.

Make an effort to walk over to a friend's house — particularly if you are both planning to watch the same film or TV show. You can then switch off the lights and turn off the heating in your house.

45. Don't splurge on paint.

Measure any surface you plan to paint carefully before you buy materials. Most people end up buying far too much paint, which then just goes to waste.

46. Get pets snipped.
Unless you want to have to deal with extra four-legged friends, get your cat or dog spayed or neutered.

47. Throw out confetti.
Use a biodegradable version
of confetti — either an
eco-friendly version from a
specialist shop, rice, or petals
and leaves from your garden.

48. Wake up and smell the chlorine.

If you do have to buy detergents or cleaners, then try and choose one that is chlorine-free, as chlorine is bad news for the environment.

49. Get a slab of green.
If you're thinking of laying a patio, opt for reclaimed bricks or stone, ideally from somewhere local.

50. Refuse refuse.

Only use recycled refuse sacks that can break down naturally in the environment.

51. Research exhaust emissions.

It's not just how efficient your car is that counts, it is also what comes out of the exhaust.

52. Don't get a cab.

Walk or take a bus whenever you can — hailing a cab can become a real habit if you're not careful.

53. Avoid parabens.

These tend to lurk in all manner of beauty products, so if you can't do without make-up, then at least check the label and steer clear of anything with parabens and petrochemicals in them.

54. Have a green wedding.

If you're planning on getting married, plan your day to be eco-friendly. Keep guests to a minimum, and arrange a venue that minimises the distances that friends and relatives have to travel.

55. Get your school involved.
If you're at school or have
children at school, contact the
headmaster to see what they
can do to help the environment.
The most eco-friendly schools
offer fair trade organic school
uniforms — try and persuade
your school to do so too.

56. Get informed.

Keep up-to-date with the latest facts about climate change so that whenever the subject comes up in discussion you can persuade others how easy it can be to adopt a greener lifestyle. New environmentally-friendly products and practices are being created all the time.

57. Tie a yellow ribbon.

When wrapping presents, don't use sticky tape that forces the recipient to tear open the paper to get at their prezzie. Tie the package with a ribbon or string so that the paper remains intact and can be used again.

58. Eat before you leave the house.

We tend to buy more when we are hungry, so make sure you only go shopping on a full stomach.

59. Don't buy disposable diapers.

They may be more convenient but they are much worse for the environment. Reusable diapers help the planet and will save you massive amounts of cash too. If all that dirty laundry fills you with dread, there are companies who will provide you with a fresh supply of clean diapers and take the used ones away to be cleaned.

60. Get involved.

Join a local green group and help spread the message about environmentally-friendly living.

61. Find a farmers' market.

Farmers' markets are becoming more and more popular, so check if there is one in your area. If you can buy from one of these markets you will help the environment by cutting down on transportation and packaging costs.

62. Recycle your old telephone directories.

Don't forget to recycle your old directory when a new one arrives. It is all too easy to end up with a pile of directories, so if you receive more than one type then send it for recycling.

63. Take litter home.
If any of your litter is recyclable, then bring it home with you rather than binning it when you are out and about.

64. Grow, don't mow.
Don't cut your grass too short or too frequently — longer grass is better at retaining moisture. That means you can cut down on water use in summer.

65. Convert your car.

It is often cheaper than you think to convert your gas-guzzler to run on a more environmentally-friendly fuel, such as LPG or biofuel. These fuels are cheaper as well as being cleaner, so you will easily recoup your investment if your annual mileage is high.

66. Find out what grows when.

These days you can buy most fruit and vegetables all year round — but if you buy products that are not in season locally, then you could be buying something shipped in from the other side of the world. So it's better yo buy locally and what's in season.

67. Get the kids involved.

If you are planning a children's party, don't be tempted to take them all to the local fast food restaurant. Host an outdoor party somewhere local and encourage the children to study and interact with their environment.

68. Plant a hedge.

If you currently have a moldering fence in the garden, consider replacing it with a hedge. Hedges provide a haven for wildlife and don't need to be treated with toxic preservatives as fences do.

69. Hire power tools.
Before you rush out and purchase the latest power tool, consider how often you are realistically going to use it. You can hire most tools for a fraction of the cost or borrow them from a friend or neighbor.

70. Grow garlic.

Garlic plants repel many garden pests (which will allow you to cut back on chemical pest control products) and have many uses in the kitchen.

71. Don't forget to recycle cardboard.

In general cardboard can be recycled — even if your local collection scheme warns you to only put out paper and plastic. Find out where your local cardboard bank is, and take all your old boxes and containers to it.

72. Get to know your local retailer.

If your local shopkeeper does not stock a very wide variety of environmentally-friendly goods, let him or her know that you would buy them if they were available.

Most shopkeepers are more than happy to start stocking goods that sell!

73. Say no to free newspapers.

If you regularly receive a free local paper that you find useless, then try and collar the person who delivers it and ask them to skip your address in future. If this doesn't work, put a polite sign in your window.

74. Pump it up.

Use pump dispensers rather than aerosols whenever you can. Remember to refill your pump dispenser rather than throwing it away.

75. Exclude drafts.

You can make your own draft excluders for a truly green option — but even if you have to buy some they are a worthwhile investment as they will prevent cold air getting in and warm air getting out.

76. Don't impulse buy.

Make a pledge never to buy something at the same time as you first spot it in the shop. Instead, go away and think about whether you really need the product. You may find that the next day it does not seem quite such a 'must-have'.

77. Don't sprinkle.

Sprinkler systems waste huge amounts of water, so use a watering can or a garden hose instead.

78. Fall in love with hemp.

Hemp is a great environmentally-friendly alternative to cotton, so look out for products made from it. These days there are many hemp products including clothes and bed linen.

79. Befriend your neighbors.

If your neighbors know your habits and when you are away on holiday, they can keep an eye on your house so that you won't need to invest in energy-hogging security lights. There are many other resources that can be shared to save time and money.

80. Fit a catalytic converter.
If you have an older car, then
fitting a catalytic converter
can dramatically reduce your
car's emissions.

81. Organize a 'walking bus'.

Take your kids to school the greenest way possible — walk. Arrange a route that will allow several sets of children to be picked up along the way and form a 'crocodile' so that no-one gets lost on the route.

82. Terrace your garden.

If you have a garden with a marked slope, then install terraces to prevent the rain running off. This will help reduce the need for watering.

83. Limit your lawn.

Keep the amount of space you devote to your lawn relatively small, and plant hardy plants in containers and rock gardens. Choose plants that can survive in a variety of conditions, rather than ones that rely on constant watering.

84. Install a water meter.
Contact your water provider to see if they are prepared to install a water meter so you can monitor exactly how much water you are using.

85. Install a power meter.

It can be difficult to track exactly how much energy your appliances are using, but it is now possible to buy power meters that display exactly which devices are hogging resources. When you work out which ones are costing you the most money, you'll know which ones to switch off first.

86. Buy eco-paint.

If you need to repaint your walls, opt for 'eco-paints' that are free from toxic solvents. Ask your local hardware store to order some for you if they don't already stock it.

87. Believe in a flat world.

Try and favor flat pack products over assembled products. It takes far more energy to transport assembled items across the world than it does to transport ready-assembled goods.

88. Buy eggs in cardboard boxes.

Cardboard egg boxes are generally made from recycled paper which is biodegradable — this is a much more eco-friendly choice than plastic or polystyrene egg boxes.

89. Don't throw out eggshells.
Eggshells can provide a great source of calcium for your soil — crush them up and sprinkle them in the garden.

90. Water your lawn in the evening.
Water evaporates much more quickly during the day, so water at dusk or early in the morning.

91. Rake it in.

Don't use leaf blowers to get rid of fallen leaves — use a garden rake and add the leaves to your compost pile.

92. Use hedge clippers.

Manual hedge clippers are much greener than electric hedge trimmers — and they'll keep you fit too!

93. Be a weeder.
Pull weeds up by hand rather
than using weed killer. If you
can get the roots of the weeds
up it is usually more effective,
and it will provide you with
some excellent exercise too.

94. Make a fuss.

Don't sit and seethe about environmental issues — talk to the people who matter most. Shopkeepers, politicians, owners of businesses and school headmasters can all influence the planet greatly — persuade them of the case for going green.

95. Give your time as a present.

Rather than giving a loved one a gift they may not want, why not offer your time as a gift? You could help out for an hour with decorating, rubbish removal or gardening. This may be particularly welcome help for people who can't do these things themselves.

96. Make your own baby food.
Baby food tends to be hugely over-packaged due to the small portion sizes. Invest in a hand blender and make your own from organic vegetables and fruit.

97. Buy kids' clothes in slightly larger sizes.

Kids grow out of clothes all too quickly, so limit the amount of new clothes you have to buy by getting a size or two too large, then turning up trouser legs, sleeves, etc.

98. Send your specs overseas.
If you need new glasses,
ask your optician if
they run a scheme for
recycling your old ones.
Many opticians run schemes
that send old spectacles
off to poor countries.

99. Have some green gear.

Gardening can really take its toll on your clothes, so never wear regular clothes when you're doing any jobs that might cause clothes to become torn or damaged. Keep some really well-worn clothes aside especially for gardening.

100. Don't use wasteful car washes.

A commercial car wash or pressure washer uses far more water than the 'bucket and sponge' method, so when your car really does need a wash, do it yourself with a bucket of rainwater.